This book is dedicated to the following people for their inspiration and love:

Kitty Howell, Claire Curran, Margaret Walker, Darren Livingstone and all the artists at Sink the Ink Tattoo Studio. You have all inspired me to write this book of poetry.

I'd also like to say a big "love you" to Emily and Matthew Harris. For giving me back my Ready Break glow.

CONTENTS

		Page No
1	Table Three Away	5
2	Blissfully Unaware	6
3	Fitba'	7
4	Abuse	9
5	The Gramophone	11
6	And Yet	12
7	Rush Hour	13
8	Concrete Jungle	14
9	Ocean, What Ocean	15
10	A Homeless Winter	16
11	The Dram	18
12	But That's Tomorrow	19
13	The Haunting	21
14	Buzz, Buzz, Buzz	22
15	Teenage Genocide	23
16	The Record Store	24
17	The Sounds Of Calm	26
18	The Anchor	27
19	I Dinnae Get It, I Dinnae Understand	28
20	The Bee & The Buttercup	28
21	The Local	30
22	Hope	31
23	Lonely Nights	32
24	May The Force Be With You	33
25	Lazy Autumn Days	34
26	Colin Glen	35
27	An Ode To Alison	36
28	The Scrap	37
29	Alas	40
30	The Picture	41
About The Author		42

Table Three Away

-"Table three away Chef"
-"Was that a please?"
-"Eh?"
-"Two minutes!"
-"They're in a hurry Chef"
-"Two minutes!!"
-"But......."
-"Are you deaf?"
Plate carriers, 110 covers down and 120 degrees in the kitchen
Nice restaurant, neat kitchen, no extraction
CHRIST IT'S HOT!
-"Table Three away please!" Jesus where did he go? Christ it's
hot
-"I SAID TABLE FUCKING THREE AWAY !!"
I swear tae fuck
-"TABLE THREE!!!!"
-"Why's the chef shouting?
God give me strength
What a Job
What a life
What a mess
TABLE THREE, TABLE THREE, TABLE FUCKING
THREE....

Blissfully Unaware

The toilet cistern's bust
The book's gather dust
The milk in the fridge turns to mould
The body has gone cold
He lies on the floor
How long must he lie there
Before people are aware?
The mail at the door pile's high on the floor

Bottles of milk mount upon the path
Surely someone can do the math
He didn't die because of his health
He died because of his wealth
Old age pensions are not the land of milk and honey
It's lonely and deathly cold when there's not enough money
The old man died from hypothermia
He did not die from dementia
Government cuts let him down
They may as well have pulled the curtain down
His mind alive no more
He lies dead upon the floor
How long must he lie there
While people walk by blissfully unaware

FITBA'

Young boys bubble with anticipation
Into the changing rooms
"New strips the day lads"
The team run out onto the muddy pitch
A few stretches to limber up, just like the pros
They line up,two teams of young hopefuls
22 Messi's all hoping their team wins
As the whistle blows rain starts to whip across the pitch
Parents huddled together, wrapped up for the cold wet
      weather
Each secretly praying for their pride and joy to score
It would light anyone of them up like a tree at Christmas
Teams battle each other, they battle the weather together
Finally the game is over
The pitch torn up, left muddy and waterlogged
For all, victors and losers alike
Tell stories of who should've passed to who
Who missed this and who missed that
Eventually it's time for home, time for that shower
Rising steam as the warm water washes chilled dirty
      bones
At last the mud and cold have gone
Into warm jammies, sit in front of the fire, more stories
      and yarns
"If only so and so had passed I would've scored....."

All is soon forgotten though as Mum brings in hot
                chocolate and marshmallows
The coal fire sparks warmth into the room
Yawns signify sleep is not far away
Snuggling up on the couch, dreams of next week's match
come with the commentary of the sandman
"Messi passes to Matt, he beats one, shoots and scores
All is well in Slumberland

ABUSE

He awakes in darkness, his eyes puffy and sore
He had cried himself to sleep
Remembering it's not night confusion muddles his brain
Memories attack his fragile state
Pain hurts his bruised and battered body
Awareness of time has come and gone
Could it be at least two hours even more
Since he last saw daylight
Locked in under the stairs
Trying to move his legs pain causes him to wince
Scared to make a sound in case he's still mad
As time goes on the agony intensifies
There's a wetness in and around his crotch
It feels like the floor is wet
Hand down the back of his pants
Panic stricken as he realises the sticky fluid is blood
Scared, frightened and in shock
That so called man beat him unconscious
She just watched, a wicked grin, her evil smoked stained teeth
appearing like a foggy smothered sun
"I don't like carrots" Cheeky ungrateful little fucker she spat
Eventually the key turns, light streams in
Rays of light hurt his eyes
What's the grown up word, irony
For there is no sunshine in his life

HOPE

When there is it hurts
Man of evil he calls father screams an order
He crawls out of the cramped cupboard hoping he heard right
He tries to stand, his legs crumble like a newborn foal trying
        to grasp it's balance
Blood stained trousers mark the carpet
The evil witch screams, grabs his hair and drags him to his
        room
No T.V, no going out to play, no love, no normal life for this
        boy of ten
Frightened to fall asleep, for sleep brings another day
Another day, another beating
He stands on uneasy legs
One step at a time he makes the painful journey to the
        window
Opening the window the gust of cold air stings his raw skin
He climbs up on the sill and holds on
Blood pisses down his leg
He no longer fears the devil for the devil is downstairs
The devil can harm no more
He steps off and out into the night sky

THE GRAMOPHONE

Taking the old 78 out it's fusty smelling sleeve
With gentle hands it's lain on the turntable
Winding the handle round, picking up speed, the anticipation
builds
Lifting the needle onto the record it's vinyl begins to crackle
Music of a humbled generation as Billie sings Strange Fruit
This beautiful antique started it all
From Gramophone to Mono to Stereo and on
Progression demands for the perfect sound
Now with Ipod this and MP3 that, downloading is what it's all
about
Oh wonderful gramophone who guided music of older
generations into the present
Rooms filled with your wonderful melodious sounds
So take a bow old fella
For without you to lead the way
Our World would have been a sadder, lonely and darker place

AND YET

This mental torture I keep putting myself through
I can't take much more
Images of another man with a woman I once loved
A concoction of pills and Whisky are whispering my name
Isolation row is a hell of a place to be
I've fought and fought but now exhaustion has rested in my
        mind
My ideas of life have slipped out the back door
Denis Wilson sings 'Farewell My Friends'
Is this time, the time to travel to my journeys end
The thread of life is fraying
The thread of death is turning to rope pulling at my rotten
        core
Twisting and turning, round and round
Sick of kidding myself on
There's nothing left
I've nothing left
Raped of self belief, raped of hope, raped of all emotion
Death feels like my only solace
And yet.......

Rush Hour

Impatient drivers sit all revved up with nowhere to go
Rush hour traffic, cars bumper to bumper
"PLEASE SOMEBODY MOVE !"
Commuters line the pavements all in a rush to get somewhere
       they don't want to be
Jack Frost attacks those who dare to bare skin in the name of
       fashion
Hot air emancipates from frozen bones hitting the cold
Puffs of steam could mistake them for angry bulls ready to
       gorge and stampede
Stepping into the warmth dense heat hits them like Ali's right
       hook
Tingling as the cold leaves the body
Off to mug some other patch of bare skin
Traffic has begun to ebb and flow Pavements quieter now
Bedlam ruled only fifteen minutes ago
Ghost town vibes hit the city
Staff look out of windows, bored, waiting
Long time till lunch time
The air has warmed under the winter sun
Blue skies like ice surround all
Normality returns at the death of rush hour

CONCRETE JUNGLE

"I'm a thumbprint on a skyscraper"
He heard that once
Through tears of despair the quote stabs at his loneliness, his
          fears, his depression,
His own feeling of insignificance
Summed in that one line
Not being able to fight
His willingness to live is slipping away
Time consumed energy of abject failure releases more
          negativity
Loved ones gone like a puff of a smoke
Still the memories attack
Ones filled with love, ones filled with vile hatred
He has to get out of this flat smothered in gloom
Wasted energy leaves him motionless
If there is no movement soon
Suicide awaits patiently with open arms
His body still like concrete
His mindset drowned in concrete
To live is to move, is to dress, is to wander towards the door
The concrete cracks......

Ocean, What Ocean?

I met you once, seems like a lifetime ago
When you found out I was ill you were there
Messenger back and forth
Quicker than the pony express
Images of you, sunglasses on
Driving in the Floridian sun
Hair flowing and that smile that affects everyone
Here am I on the other side of the ocean
I look forward to your messages with anticipation
Like a child who's been well behaved
The reward, a trip to the sweet shop
You worried when I was sick
I worried when you had your scan
You interrupt my loneliness with tales of laughter
I interrupt your headaches with innuendo
We embarrass each other
I'm lucky to call you my friend
My loving American friend the Atlantic seems so small with
        you in my life
Ocean, what ocean?

Homeless Winter

Alone, destitute, cold
The doorway shelters me from the biting wind
Torn up cardboard box is my bed for the night
It's not too bad, I have a blanket for comfort
I snuggle in and try to cut the noises of the night from my
        mind
In a few more weeks the frost will come along with
hypothermia and frostbite
Heaven comes in the shape of a van, round midnight
The hot soup warms the blood
It's not too long before the chill sets into these auld bones
In winter every morning you wake is a prayer answered
No one knows when this bitter cold will take your life
Days are not much better
Trying to stay warm while belittling your dignity begging for
        pennies
People in their warm clothes look at you like you're the shit
        on their new shoes
No one knows your story nor do they care
You are already labeled
Junkie, Drunk, Freak, Christ even been called paedo
I'm none of the above
I'm cold, I'm hungry, I'm unfortunate
I yearn for warm shelter, Hot Food, Hot Bath as I wander off
        to the shelter

16

HOPE

At least for an hour I'll be warm and have a hot meal
After, It's back to begging I go
Hoping Global Warming does me a favour this winter
My body is old, My body is tired, My body is frozen
If it's as cold as last year I'm afraid Winter will take me into
       it's fold

THE DRAM

Breaking the seal of an 18 year Malt brings only anticipation
Your mouth begins to salivate with excitement
You can keep your Chateau De Vinegrate
The bottle held up to the light surrenders the liquid heaven
Twisting the cork it squeaks out it's prison
Surrendering smells of smoked oak barrels and peaty bogs
First the Whisky glass, the clinking of three ice cubes
Another smell brings visions of rutting Stags, antlers clashing
          on fields of purple heather
Silently it pours itself from the bottle
Ice cubes crack under the strain of it's warmth
Let it sit for minute, savour the moment
The ice melts like global warming attacking Antarctica
Another snifter, Images of the Highlands come to mind
At last with mouth watering tastebuds, a wee shoogle of the
          glass
Lifting it up, quivering lips take a sip
Your mouth comes alive with Ceilidhs, mountains covered in
          snow
Another sip reminds you of Bracken, The Highland
Clearances and of plump Grouse feeding on grains of Barley
Smokey barrels left empty and alone to rot with damp,
eventually to waste away
Do not mourn their death
For what's left behind is the barrel's bloodline
The Dram.....

But That's Tomorrow

The darkness has seeped its way into his mind
His body sags with the weight of his world
Lifting his legs to reach for Whisky and Diazepam to numb
his aching bones
Soon his eyelids will get heavy
A glaze of alcohol and prescription drugs take hold
Willie V sings "I've Fucked Up Again"
A sardonic grin crosses his face, like a small child crossing a
busy road, scared of oncoming traffic
He fights the state of comatose coming over him
"Drink Drugs Man, The ultimate stone"
The stone of death for some
Fucking hippies, if only they knew the reality
Stoned, drunk, but fuck man this ain't no high
The abject misery brings tears
Feeling the pain of Willy's voice
Man's half way round the world doesn't know him from
          Adam
Yet every lyric, every emotion sums up his downward spiral
Rolling off the couch the floor hits him with a dig
Lying on his battered back looking at the blurred ceiling
He laughs hysterically, manically
Laughter turns to sobbing
He crawls to bed "Where the fuck is the bed ?"
No control anymore darkness smothers him

Later he wakes, cold, smelling rancid and damp
"Ah fuck it" he mumbles
Standing, he stumbles then falls
"Christ I'm like fucking Bambi on stilts"
Trying to take his pish stained pants off
He falls again, cracking his head
Laughter of the desperate fills the air,
"I've Fucked Up Again" ringing in his ears
Bloodied head he conks out
Tomorrow will bring another day of desperation
Another day to fight
Another day to surrender
Another day to hang on for dear life
But that's tomorrow....

HOPE

The Haunting

Awakening with a jump
His heart pounding, his head thumping
What in the fuck is going on?
Skeletal faces flashing in and out
Bed clothes soaked in sweat
Was he drowning?
Is he drowning in the fear of sleep?
Darkness mummifies his fears
Standing he begins to shake
Sodden pyjamas make it hard to walk
A whisper touches the back of his neck
Was it a breeze? A voice?
He collapses back onto the bed
Faces scream into his mind
Head in hands he sobs, wailing like a Banshee at a wake
Rising he leaves the bed of nightmarish hell
No more sleep tonight
The demons have departed
Left their pain and sorrow
Off to haunt some other hapless soul
In the night of unforgiving dreams

Buzz Buzz Buzz

Walking through the door the buzzing of guns
Artists work their magic
Human canvasses take the pain
Skin red raw, some bloodied
Still the buzzing goes on
Like demented wasps on cocaine
First comes the stinging
Then the pain, The numbness
Each canvass puts on a brave face
Concentration etched on the artist
No room for mistakes here
Finally you're done
The work of art hypnotises
Stunning, Beautiful, Fucking Awesome
Still the demented wasps buzz on....

For Darren Livingstone and all at Sink Ink, Belfast

TEENAGE GENOCIDE

This used to be the area where we lived, where we hung
        around
In came the developers and tore it down
"Apartments" for the rich looking to buy property
If we want to live there now we'd have to win the fucking
        lottery
We're put into damp housing that the council call schemes
They beat us down with these tiny flats, Try to take away our
        dreams
Society and the Media screams we have no respect
You took away our houses WHAT THE FUCK DID YOU
        EXPECT?
Crack, Alcohol, Speed, Rock and Heroin
It's like our Generation have all gave in
Depression, Panic, Fear and Suicide
Nothing to do, Has left us with Teenage Genocide.....

The Record Store

Many many years ago every town had one
Through the progression of time they all disappeared
It's time for a comeback
With vinyl being the partner in crime they will take on the
        world once more
A Phoenix from the ashes
This has past myth status, This is legendary
New stores have Re-releases, Repressed with digital sound
Surely to Jesus H Christ they're missing the point
Opening the door of a great record store
The first thing that hits is the smell
The fustiness of the old second hand sleeves
Excitement does drum rolls in your stomach
Rows of albums await inspection
Flicking through like a crazed madman
A to Z and back again
Only at C and ten albums down
Can these prices be right? Fuck I'm going to have a meltdown
A bargain here, a bargain there
What is that playing?
Elvis Costello, American Import from '78, Only five quid!!
Fuck, Fuck, Fuck
Keep calm, great nick, keep calm
Up to the counter with your haul
Deep breath, Ya beauty right prices

Into brown paper bags
Money exchanged without a flinch
Chat with other vinyl heads
This band that band, no not mumford and sons or Ed
        Sheeran
Still the grooves crackle and spin
The magical sound fills the store as you step outside and close
        the door...

THE SOUNDS OF CALM

Lying under a palm tree

Looking at sailboats motionless on top of a still sea

On the bed of the Gulf, Crustaceans and various Fish vie for
their small piece of watery desert

Was this what it was like for Hemmingway when he wrote

The Old Man And The Sea

Islands dotted around, overgrown in an orgy of trees and
bushes

Basking in the shade, An Iguana runs into it's own safe haven

Trees come alive with the sound of Crickets and Insects

Noises spread all around

Then nothing!

All returns to a peaceful serenity

Gentle lapping of waves as they finally make their destination

Washing up on golden sands

Not for long though as the Tide dictates It's time to move on

A different adventure, maybe a different Ocean

The last few nights the old wooden piers have stood their
ground

As The Gods Of Thunder pounded them with their anger and
sound

For now though all is quiet under a hot afternoon sun...

THE ANCHOR

Drowning in a sea of despair
Lost, confused, alone
Suicidal thoughts, depression, anxiety circling like Great
       Whites
I needed you to throw a lifeline
Rescue me from the demons before it was too late
Instead you threw me an anchor
No compassion, No understanding
"Me, Me, Me" was all I could hear
As I sank deeper into my despair the Great Whites began to
       feed
Death appeared more than once flashing its teeth
Still the anchor pulled me down further into the abyss
As I lay at the bottom, alone, drowning
Lungs filled with self doubt, self hatred, self pity
Life started to seep from my worthless body
Visions of a new beginning appeared
I broke the anchor
I swam for dear life, for new hope
Reaching the surface I gulped the air of future happiness
My lifeboat of self belief sailed away
Your anchor lay on the ocean bed
Rusting with your corrosive tongue....

I Dinnae Get It, I Dinnae Understand

We had the chance by Democratic vote to get the English
        oppressors off our land
We went to the polls in our droves, we said 'no'
I dinnae get it, I dinnae understand
Westminster still rules us, nuclear weapons upon our land
Still we said 'no'
I dinnae get it, I dinnae understand
We let the media, ruled by an Australian, influence the minds
        of the people
Underhand tactics by Cameron as he wheeled in Brown
He told us 'no' letting us down once more
I dinnae get it, I dinnae understand
Economists said we had the resources to survive
With oil in our seas and gold in our mountains
The corporate companies said they would leave
Why did we no call their bluff
I dinnae get it, I dinnae understand
Things kept getting worse
After, an election was called
87% voted for our Nationalist Party but England ruled with
        the Tory vote once again
I dinnae get it, I dinnae understand
Food Banks become more by the day
Westminster retains its grip
We voted 'yes' but it was too late
I dinnae get it, I cannae understand

THE BEE & THE BUTTERCUP

A summers sun brightens all around
It's at it's highest this time of day
Shade from the trees doesn't bring a much well needed breath
of air
A ray of light breaks through the trees
Buttercups turn from their buttery yellow to bright white as
the light catches them unaware
For one shaded buttercup there is no light
The deep yellow and It's perfumed smell of pollen attracts an
admirer
Hovering above is a busy buzzing Bee
Wings beating 600 to the second, faster than Bonzo's drum
solos
He flies around the cup once then twice
Satisfied there are no conflicts of interest
Bertie Bee lands and settles into the cup
Pollen is extracted by the Busy Bee
The Buttercup gives no resistance
Sunshine breaks through brightening up the flower
As the greedy wee Bee has had his full he settles down for a
nap
A Pillow provided by the Golden petals
Summer is here for the Bee and The Buttercup

THE LOCAL

Wandering into my local
The Barman has already started pouring
Shit day at work behind me
Guinness ¾'s poured sits settling
A few more of the lads walk in
Chat turns to last night's Hurly
The banter begins, the noise levels rise
"That's 25 Euros please"
"Away and fuck off! I only ordered a pint"
"Bhoys said it was your round"
Bastards! Here we go, I feel a sesh coming on
Couple of guys start up the fiddly dee
Creamy pints of stout are passed over
The musicians smile, they can smile all they want
Game's on the night and we're watching it!
'Black Is The Colour' laments through the bar
A Donal Lunny tune next
Roars of applause fill the noisy bar
"Nae Fitba' the night lads"
Pints flow, musicians hit their groove
Sound down, Fitba' on, better than nothing
No one really cares, music wins the night over
Looking around I smile
Work! What the fuck's work?
The craic, the swallae, the music, worriers bah!
Locals are made for days like these....

HOPE

The envelope of darkness is beginning to crush my soul to
     sleep
The Inevitable does not seem far now
My mind rapes my past, looking for hope
A glimmer of light, anything to shine
Through the self pity of misery
There is nothing, no smiles of distant memories
I lie here a lumpen mass of worthlessness
I fear death is closer now
I accept it's rotten core of inevitability
There is no hope, there is no fear
I will soon be from my madness
In the darkness my mind and body will rot
My soul will rise into the light
Where yarns of old will be told
From them glimpses of hope will take hold....

LONELY NIGHTS

Looking into my Guinness stained glass, I see your reflection
Your face shines in the mirror of its blackness
I look around but you're not there
Where did it go wrong?
This love that was once so strong
I sit in this pub with you in my mind
Time to get bladdered
The shout goes up " Last Orders "
Ach well that's put paid to that
I finish up
As I wander out into the rainy streets
Strains of "I'll Never Fall In Love Again" follow me out into
      the pouring rain
Fat chance pal, Fat chance...

May The Force Be With You

My dark forces wrap their self around me
I'm constrained in a shrouded blanket of death
I twist and turn in my straight jacket
Unlike Houdini I can't escape it's locked keys of torment
The jacket tightens squeezing my mind of all common sense
If there's a way to live and let live I can't find it
Ian Fleming's Live And Let Die pops into my head
I've lived my life despite It's faults
I lived It well and despite these thoughts wriggling around
The Jacket loosens, The Blanket slips but the locks won't snap
I won't die tonight, It's a small fight won
There will be harder to come
Eventually one day I will loose
Death will take It's toll
My forces will be with me as long as I fight
Doctor Death waits in the wings, watching, smiling while
        rubbing his skeletal hands....

LAZY AUTUMN DAYS

The Day has dragged by
Listening to the sound of the brook
Whistling wind makes music with the accompanying trees
Leaves fall to the sodden ground
Skeletons of summer are left behind
Winter will be here soon
For now Autumn fights on
Mist crawls over the hills
Soon to smother the view with it's pristine white blanket
Rain pelts the double glazing
It's good to be inside
The warmth of the room makes me sleepy
I curl up on the couch as the Sandman lets himself into the
        room
Bringing dreams of lazy Autumn days......

COLIN GLEN

The wood yawns itself awake
Streams of sunlight flood through the thickets
A slight breeze aids the trees to rub and sway together
Creaking like an oiled door hinge, looking like an
        Hermaphrodite
Dancing fairies play, rabbits hop from burrow to burrow
Mother Nature is on the decks as the volume of forest life
        comes alive
Robins, Chaffinch, Blue Tits and Blackbirds chirp their lines
        in the feathery choir
Buzzards glide across the sky, silent assassins looking for prey
Forest light grows stronger
Vibrant greens come alive
Wild garlic leaf perfume the air
The babbling creek adds it's thunderous baritone to the
        feathery choir
Moss, ivy, bark, young buds of Spring paint the wood with
        colour
Snow Drops pop up like pearls of wisdom
And the morning dew sits on top of it all
The woods varnish gives it a Mr. Sheen glean
A glean which reflects the picturesque life and hope of Spring
A new gift for life for all who reside there
New life will bring eternal hope for the future seasons ahead
In our wood called Colin Glen.....

An Ode To Alison

Images of long ago
Long brown hair, turned up jeans, Doc Martin Boots
My love lived there for a time
Eventually died there too
Years have since passed
Through ups and downs our friendship remains with mental
    scars to carry
Seems we haven't drifted that far apart
Our demons haunt us in different ways
Bringing us together to unite in our fight
Demons will eventually loose
Friendship will prevail, Stronger than before
In the distance goes that girl
Long brown hair, turned up jeans, Doc Martin boots......

The Scrap

It's a dark light outside
The wooded lane has a sense of foreboding
Wind blows the last of dying leaves from skeletal trees
An air of danger fills the sky
He's covered in a blanket of fear
A clearing opens into a hive of activity
Dogs running wild, barking, growling, snarling, white teeth
       bared
Children running around half naked, hitting each other with
sticks twice their size
Curtains from caravans twitch
Older women stand on their stoop, arms folded
The nattering stops, looks of wild fury are aimed at the
       stranger
One throws her half smoked butt at his feet, turns and slams
       her door
Her caravan shakes and rattles, Christ if you added a roll we'd
have Bill Haley
He tries not to smirk in his fear
Carrying on through the site for a mile or so
A feeling of uneasiness has joined his side
Rumbling noises rise into the air, filling it with anger and vile
       hatred
Fifty men or so, standing in a ring
Like Celtic stones

Strong and proud as the wind and rain bounces off their
        weather torn bodies
Most hold a bottle of Potcheen, all to a man are inhaling
        smoke
Scraggy faces show of hard times, violent times
Keeping the outside world at arms length is a full time job
A world that has never understood
Noise levels reach to a howling crescendo
Two men stand stripped to the waist
Standing in the middle of the human ring
Gladiatorial in stature, ready for battle
For centuries old scores have been settled like this
For some it's a rite into manhood
Rules simple, last man standing wins
Crouching, the warrior's circle each other looking for
        weakness
Bone crunch against bone, the violence begins
Ribs cracking, teeth gouged into flesh, bleeding knuckles, a
        broken nose
The Bloody senseless battle wears on
Both exhausted, Almost on bended knee
A sudden head butt, Teeth and Bone and Blood spurt
The loser falls to the muddy earth
The winner stands covered in blood from the lost warrior
Who has now been rolled on his side
"Don't want him losing his tongue as well", someone shouts
Roars of laughter fill the air but they all know if he dies the
Police will come. Fuck that!
No hospital for this loser, He'll be grand sure

Bare boned knuckles raised in the air as the victor stands
       triumphant
Money exchanges hands
Out cold, the defeated warrior is not the only one to lose
Dogs lick at puddles of spilt blood
Shortly all will get drunk as friends then fight as enemies such
       is the way
Morning will bring hangovers, broken bones, crusted blood
       over new scars
The howling dogs snap the stranger from his disbelief
Time to get out of here, back to the safety of his car
Watching the severe brutality, has left him drained and
       confused
One old man told him "Who needs a reason? 'Tis a grand for
       a Scrap'......

ALAS

ALAS I FEEL NO SADNESS AT YOUR DEATH
ALAS I FEEL NO JOY
ALAS I FEEL NO HATE
ALAS I FEEL NO LOVE
ALAS I FEEL CONTENT
ALAS I HAD NO CHILDHOOD
ALAS YOU ROBBED ME OF THAT
ALAS YOU FELT THE NEED TO BEAT
ALAS YOU HAD TO DRINK
ALAS I'M BRUISED FOR LIFE
ALAS YOU WERE DEAD ALONG TIME AGO
ALAS I WILL NOT SEE YOU BURN
ALAS I FEEL NO SHAME
ALAS YOU'RE ACTIONS ARE TO BLAME
ALAS I WISH I COULD MOURN FOR YOU
ALAS I FEEL NO SCOURNE
SO NOW YOU LEAVE YOUR WICKED WORLD
ALONE AND ABANDONED
ALAS YOU HAVE NO ONE TO BLAME BUT
YOURSELF....

The Picture

I sit and stare and ponder over your picture
Your Specs perched upon your head
A whisper of hair reaches down and gently touches the soft
        skin of your face
Those Hazel Eyes maybe dark but they light up any room
Your infectious smile
Cheeky wee Dimples
Pangs of love stab at my aching heart
It may sound like sadness, Loneliness even
It is not My Love
This picture I kiss every night
This picture I kiss every morning
It lights up My Day
It lights up My Life
It lights up the path I must travel to be with you
This picture of you that's by my side..........

To Kitty xx

About The Author

Originally from Prestwick in Scotland, Mark Evison has been living in Belfast for the past 10 years.

After suffering from mental health problems, Mark's counsellor suggested that he began writing. Throwing himself into the worlds of poetry and short stories, Mark shared his creations with his close friends who encouraged him to pursue publishing his collection.

Influenced by the likes of Charles Bukowski, John Steinbeck, Seamus Heaney and Patrick Magill, Mark brings life's ordinary experiences into an exciting and innovative light.

Now, working on a journal and collection of short stories, Mark always has a story to tell. He continues to create poetry, with enough poems to fill several more collections.